GRAPHIC LIBRARY™

GRAPHIC HISTORY

THE FIRST MOON LANDING

by Thomas K. Adamson

illustrated by Gordon Purcell and Terry Beatty

Consultant:
Roger D. Launius
Chair, Division of Space History
National Air and Space Museum
Smithsonian Institution
Washington, DC

Raintree

www.raintreepublishers.co.uk
Visit our website to find out
more information about
Raintree books.

To order:
☎ Phone 0845 6044371
🖷 Fax +44 (0) 1865 312263
🖳 Email myorders@raintreepublishers.co.uk

Customers from outside the UK please telephone +44 1865 312262

Raintree is an imprint of Capstone Global Library Limited, a company incorporated in England and Wales having its
registered office at 7 Pilgrim Street, London, EC4V 6LB – Registered company number: 6695582

Text © Stone Arch Books 2007
First published in the United Kingdom by Capstone Global Library 2010
Paperback edition first published in the United Kingdom by Capstone Global Library 2011
The moral rights of the proprietor have been asserted.

Designer: Bob Lentz
Colourist: Otha Zackariah Edward Lohse
Editor: Donald Lemke
UK Editor: Vaarunika Dharmapala
Originated by Capstone Global Library Ltd
ᵃnd bound in China by South China Printing Company Ltd

Photo credit: p. 29 Shutterstock (Taipan Kid)

ISBN 978 1 406214 33 8 (hardback)
14 13 12 11 10
10 9 8 7 6 5 4 3 2 1

ISBN 978 1 406214 38 3 (paperback)
15 14 13 12 11
10 9 8 7 6 5 4 3 2 1

British Library Cataloguing in Publication Data
A full catalogue record for this book is available from the British Library

Disclaimer
All the Internet addresses (URLs) given in this book were valid at the time of going to press. However, due to the dynamic
nature of the Internet, some addresses may have changed, or sites may have changed or ceased to exist since publication.
While the author and publishers regret any inconvenience this may cause readers, no responsibility for any such changes can
be accepted by either the author or the publishers.

Editor's note: Direct quotations from primary sources are indicated by a yellow background.

Direct quotations appear on the following pages:
Page 5, from President John F. Kennedy's Special Message to the Congress on Urgent National
    Needs on 25 May 1961, as transcribed at the John F. Kennedy Library and Museum Online
    (http://www.jfklibrary.org/Historical+Resources/Archives/Reference+Desk/Speeches/JFK/
    Urgent+National+Needs+Page+4.htm).
Pages 10, 12, 13, 14, 16, 17, 18, 20, 21, 22, from Apollo 11 PAO Mission Commentary
Transcript (http://www.jsc.nasa.gov/history/mission_trans/apollo11.htm).

CONTENTS

CHAPTER 1
THE SPACE RACE

On 4 October 1957, the Soviet Union launched a satellite called Sputnik into orbit. It was the first human-made object in space.

The news shocked Americans.

Look! That must be Sputnik.

I can't believe the Soviets have better technology than we do.

Now they can drop bombs on us from all the way across the ocean.

Sputnik spurred the US government to create an agency for space exploration. The National Aeronautics and Space Administration (NASA) was formed in 1958.

Shepard listened to Kennedy's speech with other astronauts.

Difficult?! It's impossible!

Kennedy would never have said it, if he didn't believe we could do it.

I agree. We could go to the Moon in eight years.

If we weren't competing with the Soviets, we wouldn't be going anywhere.

NASA spent the next few years testing spacecrafts. During the Mercury missions, astronauts went to space on test flights.

They performed their first space walks during the Gemini missions.

Then, NASA began Project Apollo. In December 1968, the *Apollo 8* mission made history. It carried the first astronauts around the Moon and back.

A month later, Deke Slayton met with astronauts Michael Collins, Buzz Aldrin, and Neil Armstrong. As head of the astronaut office, Slayton assigned crews to Apollo missions.

We need to stay ahead of the Soviets. After two more missions, *Apollo 11* will be the one.

If 9 and 10 go perfectly, you'll get first crack at landing on the Moon.

Thank you for your confidence in us, Deke.

We'll be ready.

NASA
Armstrong

NASA
Collins

NASA
Aldrin

The *Apollo 9* and *Apollo 10* test flights did go perfectly. NASA set the *Apollo 11* launch for July.

CHAPTER 2
TO THE MOON

During the next six months, the three astronauts spent hundreds of hours practising for the mission. Finally, on 16 July 1969, they climbed aboard the *Saturn V* rocket at Kennedy Space Center in Florida.

Nearly 500 million people around the world were watching on television.

They say the *Saturn* rocket is 110 metres tall.

Most of it is fuel.

Amazing!

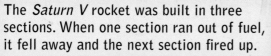

The *Saturn V* rocket was built in three sections. When one section ran out of fuel, it fell away and the next section fired up.

BBWEEEEE

RROOAARR!

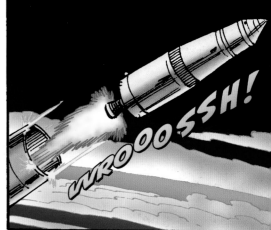

VVROOOSSH!

BBRAAAOOOOMMM!!.

On 19 July 1969, the rocket flew around to the other side of the Moon. *Apollo 11* would be out of communication range with Mission Control.

Houston, this is Armstrong. We're getting ready for loss of signal. See you in 48 minutes.

Starting engine burn now.

While out of communication range, the astronauts fired up the engine to slow down and allow the Moon's gravity to capture the rocket.

Mission Control waited to find out if the engine burn was successful.

Apollo II, this is Houston. How did the burn go?

Perfectly.

Armstrong and Aldrin had trouble hearing commands from Mission Control. Collins relayed messages to them.

Eagle, Houston. If you read, you're Go for powered descent.

Okay.

Eagle, this is *Columbia*. They just gave you a Go for powered descent.

COLLINS

Understood. We'll burn engines in three minutes.

Three, two, one . . .

Ignition!

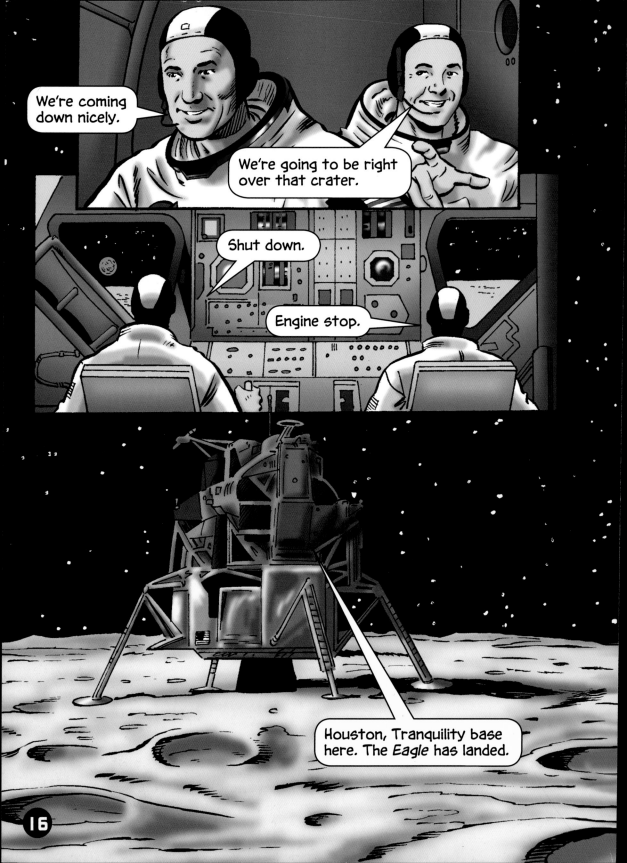

There was no time to celebrate. The flight controllers had only one minute to make sure *Eagle* was okay. If anything was wrong, the craft would have to lift off immediately.

The flight controllers quickly determined that *Eagle* and its computer were in good shape.

Eagle, you have a Go for extended surface operations.

Be advised that there are a lot of smiling faces in this room and all over the world.

It sure sounded great from up here.

You guys did a fantastic job.

Thank you. Just keep that orbiting base ready for us up there now.

Now that they knew they'd be spending some time on the Moon, the two astronauts took a good look out of the windows. Armstrong described the scene to controllers in Houston.

We're on a level plain with lots of craters. It's pretty much colourless, sort of a chalky grey.

It must be a beautiful sight.

Do you feel like sleeping for the next seven hours like you're supposed to?

Yeah, right. And try to tell kids to sleep in on Christmas Day!

Even after their long day, Armstrong and Aldrin decided to prepare for the Moon walk. They helped each other into their bulky space suits.

19

Before going down the ladder, Armstrong opened a hatch that exposed a TV camera. This camera would show the world his first steps on the Moon.

Okay, Neil, we can see you coming down the ladder now.

That's one small step for man . . .

. . . one giant leap for mankind.

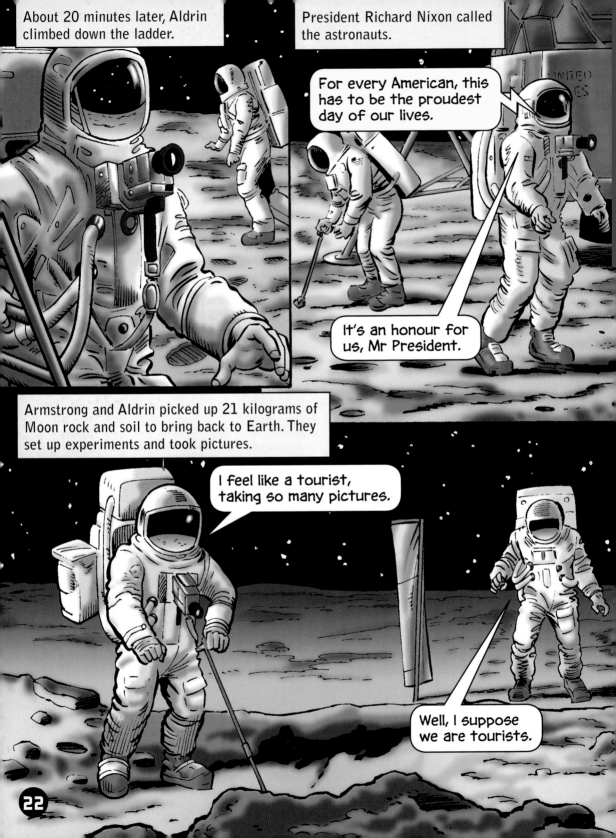

On the last day of the historic flight, the astronauts spoke to the world on television.

This mission is a symbol of the human need to explore the unknown.

We'd like to say thank you to the thousands of people who worked to make this mission a success.

CCCRRREEEEEEEE

On 24 July 1969, eight days and three hours after beginning their trip, the rocket sped back towards Earth.

When will we know if they made it through re-entry?

In a few minutes.

Look, there are the parachutes!

MORE ABOUT APOLLO 11

 Near the end of their flight, the *Apollo 11* astronauts thanked the thousands of people involved in their historic mission. In fact, about 400,000 people working on the US space programme helped make the mission a success.

After stepping on the Moon's surface, one of Armstrong's first tasks was to collect a "contingency sample". In case the astronauts had to lift off straight away, he was to collect a small sample of Moon soil. Armstrong quickly gathered three samples and placed them in his pocket.

One month before the *Apollo 11* lift off, the Soviet Union attempted to launch an unmanned mission to the Moon. The launch failed. They made another attempt on 20 July 1969. This unmanned spacecraft crashed on the Moon.

Commander Neil Armstrong walked on the Moon for 2 hours, 31 minutes, and 40 seconds.

From lift-off to splash-down, the *Apollo 11* mission lasted 8 days, 3 hours, 18 minutes, and 18 seconds. During that time, the astronauts travelled more than one and a half million kilometres.

The astronauts left a plaque on the Moon that reads:
HERE MEN FROM THE PLANET EARTH
FIRST SET FOOT UPON THE MOON
JULY 1969, A.D.
WE CAME IN PEACE FOR ALL MANKIND

After the *Apollo 11* mission, NASA completed five more missions to different parts of the Moon's surface. The last astronauts to walk on the Moon were Eugene Cernan and Harrison Schmitt on 14 December 1972, during the *Apollo 17* mission.

Apollo 15
▽

Apollo 17
▽

Sea of
Tranquility

Apollo 14
▽

Apollo 11
▽

△
Apollo 12

△
Apollo 16

GLOSSARY

abort stop something from happening in its early stages

Congress government body of the United States that makes laws, made up of the Senate and the House of Representatives

maria large dark areas on the Moon caused by lava that has flooded into craters

module separate section that can be linked to other parts

orbit path of a spacecraft around a planet or a moon

satellite spacecraft that circles the earth. Satellites gather and send information.

Soviet Union former federation of 15 countries in eastern Europe and northern Asia

INTERNET SITES

http://www.bnsc.gov.uk/8511
The website of the British National Space Centre has some great activities and information on Earth and the Moon.

http://ygt.dcsf.gov.uk/Primary/Content.aspx?contentId=1769&contentType=3
Join the NASA Kid's Club! There are fun activities to do, and lots to learn about astronauts and space exploration.

http://news.bbc.co.uk/onthisday/hi/dates/stories/july/21/newsid_2635000/2635845.stm
This website shows you how the BBC reported the Moon landing in 1969.

READ MORE

Discovery: Space, Eileen O'Brian (Usborne, 2008)

Scientists at Work. Space Pioneers: Astronauts, Louise Spilsbury and Richard Spilsbury (Heinemann Library, 2007)

The World's Greatest: Space Vehicles, Ian Graham (Raintree, 2005)

Turning Points in History: The Moon Landing, Nigel Kelly (Heinemann Library, 2007)

BIBLIOGRAPHY

Apollo 11 PAO Mission Commentary Transcript, http://www.jsc.nasa.gov/history/mission_trans/apollo11.htm

First on the Moon: A Voyage with Neil Armstrong, Michael Collins, and Edwin E. Aldrin Jr, Neil Armstrong (Little, Brown, 1970)

John F. Kennedy Library and Museum Online, http://www.jfklibrary.org/

Men from Earth, Buzz Aldrin and Malcolm McConnell (Bantam, 1989)

Moon Shot: The Inside Story of America's Race to the Moon, Alan Shepard and Deke Slayton (Turner, 1994)

INDEX